# How To...Prepare and Preach a Sermon

## John Waller

Rector, The Brickhills and Stoke Hammond, Diocese of Oxford

## GROVE BOOKS LIMITED
RIDLEY HALL RD  CAMBRIDGE  CB3 9HU

# Contents

**Acknowledgments**

I would like to thank members of GROW for their support and encouragement, especially Liz Simpson and Phillip Tovey. I would also like to thank the participants in training courses in the Milton Keynes Christian Training Course, and the Deanery of Mursley, for their contributions to the development of this material, which was influenced in its origin by elements of both the training material for Methodist Local Preachers, and the Diocese of Oxford Portfolio for training.

**The Cover Illustration** is by Peter Ashton

**First Impression** February 2005
**ISSN** 0144-1728
**ISBN** 1 85174 584 X

# Introduction 1

*The rumours of the death of preaching seem to have been somewhat exaggerated.*

It is certainly true that the style and content of preaching is changing, as it has in fact continued to do throughout the history of the church. Today, sermons are often shorter and more informal than in earlier generations, but they certainly have not died. In most forms of church life and worship, there is still an important place for somebody to speak in order to guide and encourage the congregation to be open to God's word for them through the Bible.

Sometimes the word 'preaching' can seem off-putting, because of the way it is used in our general culture nowadays. In the news media, if a politician or other public figure is described as 'preaching,' that is usually a form of criticism, as the term is used to imply something negative about their attitude and message.

Within church life, a growing range of people have some form of authorization to preach, and there are others who occasionally, or regularly, find themselves called on to speak within the worship of their local church. Sometimes, because of an unease about lack of authorization, or training, people prefer to use other terms such as 'giving a talk,' or 'speaking.' Throughout this booklet, we will use the terms 'sermon' and 'preaching' to cover all the ways in which people may speak to the people of God gathered for worship, in relation to Scripture.

This booklet will encourage you to think about what is going on in preaching, in relation to God and the life of the church and Christian people. It will offer a detailed framework for the process of preparing a sermon, summarized in the flow chart on page 8, and suggest some alternatives to the traditional form of sermon. There are some practical guidelines for what to bear in mind when you preach, and an encouragement to continue to learn through the experience of preaching.

I hope it may be especially helpful to those who are in the early stages of learning to preach, as well as useful to those with some experience of preaching, and perhaps also to those who are regular hearers of sermons as part of their church experience. As this material arose out of training courses for ministry in the local church, it may also provide a framework for such courses.

# 2      What is Preaching?

*I expect that, if you have attended church for very long, you have probably listened to quite a lot of sermons.*

There are probably a few that stay vividly in your memory. Hopefully there are many that were quite good, even if they did not stay in the conscious memory for long. There will be some, hopefully only a few, that are memorable because they seemed particularly bad in some way. All of this experience can be a useful resource for your learning.

> ### To Think About
>
> Try to recall at least one sermon that you remember as being particularly good, and one that you remember as bad. Write a few notes about what you remember about these occasions, and what you mean by describing them as 'good' or 'bad.' What can you learn from that for your own preaching?

## Definitions

I don't expect that there is such a thing as the perfect definition of preaching, but it can be helpful to think about some possible definitions, to deepen our understanding of what preaching is. This may also help you understand more deeply your own particular style and calling as a preacher, and to appreciate the strengths and weaknesses of different preachers.

> ### To Think About
>
> Before you look at the definitions offered here, write one or more of your own definitions of preaching, in a short sentence or phrase.

Here are six different definitions,[1] not all of which I would agree with. What do you think of them?

- Rehearsing before God and the congregation the saving acts of God in Christ.
- Proclaiming Good News.
- Expounding the Bible.

- Sharing personal opinions about life and faith.
- Teaching about the Bible and Christian faith.
- Persuading people to believe what the preacher believes.

Here are some others:

- Preaching is the manifestation of the incarnate Word, from the written word, by the spoken word.[2]
- It has been said in various places that good preaching is intended to 'comfort the afflicted and afflict the comfortable.'[3]

While I like this, I would modify it to the extent of saying that preaching involves bringing God's comfort to those aspects of our lives where we are 'afflicted' or troubled, and God's disturbance to where we are too comfortable.

And here is a definition of my own:

The purpose of preaching is to enable the live encounter between the Word of God—the Bible, and the people of God—this congregation.

## The Bible and Preaching

Some of those definitions touch on the place of the Bible in preaching, and not all approaches to preaching have been grounded in the Bible. Even where preaching is based on the Bible, there may be some occasions when it is appropriate to draw on a broader range of Bible passages to address a chosen subject or theme. However, the guidance offered here rests on the assumption that a sermon will normally be developed from time spent reflecting on one or more particular Bible passages, that will also be used as the Bible readings during the worship.

## The Role of the Preacher

The question of how we use the Bible in preaching leads us to the question of how we understand the role and task of the preacher, in relation to both the biblical text, and the congregation. It is often said that there is a cultural gap between the world of the Bible and today's world, and it is a vital part of the task of the preacher to bridge this gap.[4] This is a helpful insight, as effective preaching will face the many differences between the world of a Bible passage and the world of today, but also show how the word of God can speak from the Bible to today. There are different ways of carrying out this task of 'bridging the gap,' which suggest different emphases in the role of the preacher. Some of them can be pictured as follows:

### The Preacher as Messenger

The preacher engages with the Bible text, and develops an interpretation and application which is then taken and delivered to the congregation.

### The Preacher as Guide

The preacher engages with the congregation, and introduces them to the Bible text, giving some explanation to help them understand it in its original context. Having brought the congregation to the Bible, they are left to discover their own applications to their lives.

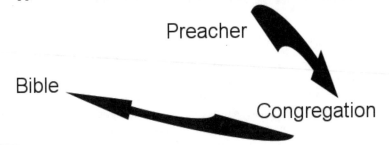

### The Preacher as Enabler

The preacher enables the engagement of the congregation with the Bible text, in the context of worship, and helps them to explore its meaning, and application to them and their lives. This reflects something of my own definition of worship, as set out above.

These models can help us to distinguish between elements that may be usefully combined in practice, and so they help us to explore some different ways of understanding the role of the preacher.

> ### To Think About
>
> Do you recognize one of these roles as representing more of the preaching you have heard, or your own style of preaching?
>
> Do you see one of them as right, or better than the others? If so, why?

There are many other possible roles for the preacher as well. Perhaps you have already thought of some. Here are some other models which have come up in group discussion:

| | | |
|---|---|---|
| Witness | Teacher | Herald |
| Wise elder | Prophet | Interpreter |
| Comforter | Challenger | Evangelist |
| Encourager | Servant | Steward |

> ### To Think About
>
> Can you think of Bible passages that suggest, or give examples of these models for somebody who speaks God's word?
>
> Or can you think of any others?

These are not exclusive, and can be combined, or adopted by the same person on different occasions. As you gain more experience in preaching, it will be useful to understand the roles that you are more gifted for, and more comfortable in, while perhaps setting out to explore one of the others from time to time.

# 3 Preparing to Preach

*Here is a flow chart which sets out an ordered series of steps in the process of preparing a sermon.*

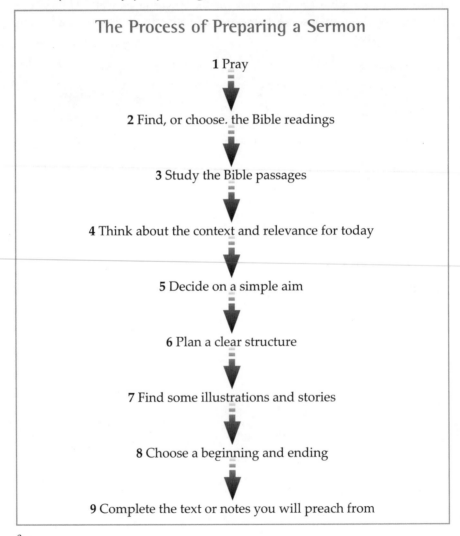

**The Process of Preparing a Sermon**

**1** Pray

**2** Find, or choose. the Bible readings

**3** Study the Bible passages

**4** Think about the context and relevance for today

**5** Decide on a simple aim

**6** Plan a clear structure

**7** Find some illustrations and stories

**8** Choose a beginning and ending

**9** Complete the text or notes you will preach from

There are various ways in which this chart could be used, or misused. If you already have some experience of preaching, you could compare the chart with your own usual pattern of preparation. This can help you be consciously aware of how you have worked in the past and so be better able to reflect on that, and decide what you are happy with and what it may be good to change and do differently in future. If you are new to preaching, the chart may give you a framework to guide you through this new, and perhaps daunting, task in the early stages, until you develop and have confidence in your own preferred pattern. This chart is not offered as a restrictive pattern to be followed laboriously in every detail, but as a guide for beginners, and a tool for reflection and continuing learning for all preachers.[5] The rest of this chapter offers some thoughts and ideas for each stage of the process.

## 1 Pray

This does not only mean praying before you do anything else, although it certainly includes that. It is also a reminder that the whole preparation process can be supported throughout by prayer. As well as the preacher praying before and during the preparation, others can be praying as well. Clergy and ministers, fellow members of a worship planning team, a church prayer group, and individual friends, are amongst those you could ask to support you in prayer. This is also an important reminder of our dependence on God's guidance. Our planning and preparation should be careful and thorough, within our practical limitations, but in the end it is all provisional, and open at any stage to God's prompting or challenge.

> **To Think About**
>
> How can you ensure that you are supported in prayer as you prepare to preach?

## 2 Find, Or Choose, the Bible Readings

As I said earlier, this pattern assumes that the sermon is developed from an exploration of the Bible readings (I will continue to refer to them in the plural, but I acknowledge that in some situations there may be only one reading). If your church follows a lectionary pattern of set readings, or plans its own scheme of readings, then you need to make sure you have the correct ones. This means knowing where to check, or who to ask, and who to talk to if you have questions or hesitations about using any of the set readings, and would like to change them. The full three year cycle of the Common Worship lectionary is included in the Common Worship main book. If you often need to refer to the lectionary, it is easier to buy the annual lectionary booklet, which is published for each church year, beginning from Advent Sunday. If you are free to choose your own readings, but are new to doing this, then perhaps you could approach a more experienced preacher for some guidance.

## 3 Study the Bible Passages

This is best done early, and given time. If possible, it can be helpful to have a first look at the readings in good time beforehand, and then let them stay in the back of your mind, while noting any thoughts or ideas that emerge, until you resume the preparation process nearer the time.

It is important to read the passages carefully, and to hear them afresh. For those who are very familiar with parts of the Bible, or who have done a lot of preaching, there can be a temptation to glance at the readings and assume you know them already, rather than taking the time to look at them properly, ready for them to speak to you anew for this particular occasion. Looking at more than one Bible translation can be helpful, as reading a passage in an unfamiliar translation can help us to hear it as if for the first time. In all this, also bear in mind whether a particular Bible translation will be used for the readings at the service when you preach.

*There can be a temptation to glance at the readings and assume you know them already*

There is not space here to look in detail at issues in biblical interpretation, but it is important that we seek to understand something of the meaning of a passage in its original context first, before going on to the next stage of applying it to our situation. Also, while our attention is mainly on the passages for a particular service, we need to retain a broader view of the whole sweep of Scripture, so that we do not see things out of proportion, or place too much emphasis on one verse or passage. Not everybody is expected to be an expert biblical scholar, but everyone who preaches has a basic responsibility to handle biblical texts in an appropriate way, and even simple insights into the background to a passage can guide and enliven its interpretation, and avoid basic errors. For example, the impact of the parable of the Good Samaritan (Luke 10.30–35) will be enhanced by an appreciation of the common assumptions about Samaritans amongst Jesus' hearers. Likewise, it is helpful to know how shocking to the religious people of his day it might be for Jesus to speak alone with the woman at the well in the way that he did (John 4.4–26).

*Bear in mind that the passage will ask questions and raise challenges for you*

One image for this part of the preparation process that may be helpful is that of a dialogue between the preacher and the Bible text. You may bring questions to the passage to help you explore its meaning, but bear in mind that the passage will ask questions and raise challenges for you and the congregation you will preach to.

Anyone who is preaching regularly will need to build up a set of basic reference books over time. If you are new to preaching, think about whom you could borrow some books from. Useful books may include ones that give a general background to the Bible, or to the Old or New Testament, and a Bible dictionary. A single volume Bible commentary may be of

*Anyone who is preaching regularly will need to build up a set of basic reference books over time*

some use, but separate commentaries on books of the Bible will contain much more detail. In time you could build up your own collection of commentaries that you will use often, while still borrowing others on some occasions. When looking for commentaries, bear in mind that Grove Books' own quarterly *Biblical Studies Bulletin* includes regular surveys of commentaries on different books of the Bible (see chapter 7 for details).

If you are working with the Common Worship lectionary, there are various books of commentary on the Principal Sunday Service readings, and other resources such as *Roots* (see chapter 7 for details), but in using these be aware of the occasional differences between the Common Worship lectionary as used by the Church of England, and the Revised Common Lectionary as used by other denominations. With any such resources, and especially those that offer outlines and ideas for sermons, it is very important to look directly at the readings first and begin to form your own ideas, before turning to them at a later stage, if at all.

---

**To Think About**

What useful books and resources do you have, or could you get access to, to help you in your preparation?

---

## 4 Think About the Context and Relevance for Today

The preacher is called to engage with the world of the Bible, and then find connections between that and the present day, and so help their hearers to do the same. Preaching takes place in a wider context, in the local context of a church and community, and within a particular act of worship. There may be particular global, national or local issues or concerns which will be significant. It is also important to be aware of the particular congregation you expect to be present at the service, and how the Bible passages may speak in a way that is relevant to their lives and faith.

Another part of the context in which you preach is yourself. Your sermon is not primarily about yourself, but it will be more effective if you can bring something of your own personality and experience to it. When your encounter with the Bible readings during preparation means that the readings have already spoken to you, this can bring more life to your preaching. There may also be other personal stories or experience that you can use to illustrate your message, so long as they are in balance with the other elements of your sermon.

*Your sermon will be more effective if you can bring something of your own personality and experience to it*

This also raises the question of when personal sharing is inappropriate. Be careful that in your sharing you do not disclose personal information about other people, in ways that are inappropriate, or that should only be done with their prior permission. There is also the issue of whether you should share your own doubts and questions in your preaching. On the one hand, honesty is important, and it is not healthy to give the appearance of a confidence and certainty that you do not feel. However, there may be some aspects of our personal experience that it would not be appropriate to share in open public worship, even if it might be possible in other settings in church life, such as a prayer group or Bible study. If you are unsure about whether to include a particular situation or experience in your preaching, it may be helpful to talk to an experienced preacher who you know, or to seek support in prayer.

---

**To Think About**

Can you think of some occasions when a sermon has been made more effective by the preacher sharing some personal experiences, or struggles?

And can you think of any occasions when you felt that some inappropriate personal sharing detracted from the impact of a sermon?

---

## 5 Decide on a Simple Aim

When I was beginning to preach, before I began my formal training for ministry, the one most helpful piece of advice I received was something like this:

Before you write a sermon, write down in one short sentence a clear aim for what you are seeking to do, and don't write anything else until you are happy with that aim.

In the early stages of my ministry I did that every time, but later the habit was formed in my thinking and I did not always write an explicit aim out. Over the years I have found it helpful to return to the discipline of doing this from time to time. If your aim consists of several sentences, or one long and complex sentence, then it is probably not well enough focussed, and needs to be shorter and sharper. It may be helpful to ask yourself the question, 'What would I like people to do as a result of hearing this sermon?', and also consider whether your aim is addressed to all of the congregation, or just to some of them.

When your early preparation has been fruitful, one of the vital skills in preaching is deciding what to leave out. If you are new to preaching, or do not preach very often, it can be tempting to try to make the most of the opportunity, and put far too much in one sermon. For any of us, it may at times be hard to set on one side something that has spoken deeply to us during our preparation, but is not relevant or appropriate to include in this sermon. However, it is actually a welcome problem to have too much material, and an idea or insight may be kept for another occasion in the future.

*One of the vital skills in preaching is deciding what to leave out*

A clear statement of your aim should be brief, but it is very important, because it is the tool you will use to test the usefulness and relevance of all the other material that will make up the sermon that you preach.

# 6 Plan a Clear Structure

Having established your aim, it is helpful to set out the structure, the main points and sequence of what you will say, before completing it all in detail. There are some structures that are often used for sermons, and it can be helpful to be aware of them. They should not be seen as limiting or restrictive, but rather as a way to appreciate a broad range of possibilities.

### Follow the Structure of the Bible Reading

This simply adopts the structure of a reading that is to be the focus of the sermon, and explains and applies it in the same order of subjects and themes as in the reading itself. This may work well with some passages, such as ones from the Old Testament prophets, or the New Testament epistles, so long as they have a clear enough theme running through them that will hold the sermon together.

### The Three Point Sermon

This is a classic sermon structure, which is also recognized in other forms of public speaking. Apart from a brief opening or conclusion, it consists of three points drawn from the reading, often with a clear logical progression from one to another. For example, a sermon based on Mary's song (Luke 1.46–55, the Magnificat) might draw out three main points to apply to our lives and faith: Mary *praises* God; Mary *trusts* that God will fulfil his promises; Mary looks for the world to *change*.

It is also possible to structure a sermon in a similar way, but with more than three points. This may work well with some readings, but experience suggests that the pattern of three points very often provides a good balance of clarity and variety.

### A Deductive Argument—from General to Particular
This has two stages, and moves from a general truth—from the Bible—to the application of that to particular or personal experience. For example, from the truth that God loves 'the world' or all people, to the assurance that God loves you and me as we are now.

### An Inductive Argument—From Particular to General
This is the opposite of the previous structure, starting from a personal or particular experience, and then connecting that with a general truth from the Bible. For example, you might begin with a true modern story of outstanding self-sacrifice of one person's life for the good of others, and then link that to the death of Jesus on the cross and its significance for all time and all people.

### A Variety of Perspectives on a Theme or Subject (sometimes called 'faceting'[6])
In contrast to the previous few structures, which follow a 'linear' logical argument from start to finish, this is almost unstructured, and consists of a variety of insights on the central theme drawn from the Bible readings. For instance, as a reflection on the passage about love in 1 Corinthians 13, you might gather a selection of thoughts, quotations, other Bible verses, stories or illustrations. This approach needs a strong central theme if it is to work well.

### A Story (or 'Narrative') Sermon
This is a sermon which does not just include one or more stories as illustrations, but consists entirely of one story, within which points are made and issues raised. For example, a sermon based on the character of Simeon (from Luke 2.25–35) could consist of an imaginative telling of Simeon's story and experience, as somebody waiting for God's promised action, and then possibly being surprised by the form that action takes. We should not be afraid to use the imagination in sermons like this, but it is important that the detail we develop never contradicts what is in the Bible passage, and that we remain aware of the distinction between what is clear from the passage, and what we imagine around it to fill out the story.

**To Think About**

Can you think of some other structures?

As you hear other people preach, are you aware of the structure of their sermons, and if so, what are they?

If you are already preaching, what structures do you tend to use most? Would it be helpful to try using some different ones?

## 7 Find Some Illustrations and Stories

Good stories and illustrations can bring a message to life, and help to make it memorable for your listeners. A sermon without any would seem very dry and theoretical, but too many could obscure your main point. As we have already noted, stories and examples from your own experience can be particularly powerful, so long as they are in balance with other aspects of the sermon, and do not disclose personal information about yourself, or other people, in a way that is inappropriate. When your meditation on the Bible passages has been fruitful, stories and illustrations may have come to mind, and these may be the most effective in your sermon. If you still need more ideas from further afield, there are a lot of possible sources for this kind of material, so this is one of the points where your aim will be important, to check that these elements serve and support your main purpose. Dramatic or entertaining stories that distract from your aim are probably not helpful.

**To Think About**

Do you find it easy to remember or think of stories and illustrations?

Are there some books or resources that could help you, or could you gradually build a collection of your own?

## 8 Choose a Beginning and Ending

The beginning of your sermon should catch the attention of your hearers, and draw them in to follow the flow of your structure. The ending needs to be clear and strong, and help to fix your main point in their minds. It is very important that a sermon only ends once. Repeated apparent endings can be very confusing and frustrating for listeners. Questions can be effective as beginnings or endings. The same phrase may be repeated as both the beginning and ending, possibly having a different or fuller meaning because of the content of the sermon. For example, one course participant offered the example of a sermon that began and ended

*Questions can be effective as beginnings or endings*

with the question, 'Have you ever been in prison?', which was drawn from the story in one of the readings, and the sermon explored various ways in which we feel trapped or confined in aspects of our lives.

If you preach in a spontaneous way, or from very brief notes, then it may still be important to plan the wording of your beginning and ending very carefully.

## 9 Complete the Text or Notes You Will Preach From

There is a wide spectrum of possibilities for what to have in front of you as you preach, from a full word-for-word text, through more or less extensive notes, to a very brief outline, or no notes at all. Unless you are already an experienced public speaker in other settings, it is probably better to work with a fairly full text or extensive notes to begin with. This may also help you to judge how long your sermon will take to deliver. However, there is a particular skill in preaching from a full script in a way that helps it come to life for your hearers. If you are used to writing reports, essays, or articles to be read by others, it will be very important to remember that preparing a text to be spoken is a different skill. Practising speaking your sermon out loud will be time well spent.

It can be useful to find out what kind of notes other preachers use, to be aware of all the possibilities, and then to work out over time what is most helpful for you. Do not let other people impose their own preferences on you. I once knew of somebody who had been told to preach without any notes, but this caused them some problems, as they were easily distracted, and lost the thread of their argument. I believe that they would have got on better by having some outline notes or headings, to fall back on if necessary.

Whatever you have with you on paper or card, whether hand-written or printed, it needs to be large enough for you to read, easy for you to follow, and, if it is on more than one sheet, easy to keep in the right order.

---

*To Think About*

If you are new to preaching, what kind of text or notes will you use to begin with?

If you are an experienced preacher, has your style of text or notes changed over time? Are you happy with what you do now, or could you try something different?

---

# Alternative Approaches

# 4

*There are many other ways of bringing the word of God to life in the worship of the church, as well as the traditional approach of one person standing and talking.*

Everything in this booklet so far has assumed that the sermon will consist of one person speaking, but there are many other possibilities. Depending on our own gifts, and the contexts in which we preach, we may use these other approaches frequently, or very rarely, but it is important to be aware of them.

---

### To Think About

Before you look at the list that follows, can you think of any occasions when you have experienced the word of God explored in worship by some means other than a traditional sermon (whether you were taking part, or leading)?

What did you think of them?

Do you have other ideas that you have not yet tried out, or experienced?

---

During different courses I have been involved in, participants have suggested many ideas, including these:

◆ Several 'mini-sermons' integrated within the pattern of the service

◆ Story telling

◆ Visual aids to emphasize the main points of the sermon (a librarian was used to using a 'story sack' of objects to show as they spoke or told a story)

◆ Conversation or dialogue between two speakers

◆ A group of people planning and giving the sermon together

◆ Drama sketches based on readings or the sermon theme

◆ Testimony or personal story-telling (perhaps through an interview)

♦ A quiz based on the readings

♦ Video or computer projection of key words, or images

♦ Movement or activity involving the congregation

♦ Group discussion by the congregation:

- in response to the Bible readings

- in response to the sermon (perhaps with some questions for discussion)

- to prepare questions to ask the preacher, or others

If you feel uncomfortable with some or all of this diverse range of possibilities, it is also worth noting some of the guidance in the introduction to *A Service of the Word*.[7]

> Telling (the Christian) story and expounding it in the 'sermon' can be done in many different and adventurous ways…The word 'sermon' is used in the service, and explained in the note, precisely because it would be too limiting to use words like 'address,' 'talk,' 'instruction,' or 'meditation.'
>
> The term 'sermon' includes less formal exposition, the use of drama, interviews, discussion, audio-visuals and the insertion of hymns or other sections of the service between parts of the sermon.

Much of the advice given in the previous chapter can still be applied to these alternative approaches, and establishing the aim of the 'sermon' may be especially important, so that it can be used to test the helpfulness of ideas for a particular occasion.

---

*To Think About*

Is there at least one new idea, however big or small in scale, from this chapter or your own thinking, which you could try out in your preaching in the near future?

---

# On the Day

# 5

*You may have your text or notes prepared and ready, but there are still a lot of other points to bear in mind on the day when you give your sermon.*

## Practical Points

You may be very familiar with the place where you will preach your sermon, but if you have not preached before, or are going somewhere for the first time, then there are various points it will be useful to keep in mind, and check beforehand if you can. These may include:

- How does the sermon fit in with the rest of the service? (especially if you are not leading the service)

- How are you expected to begin or end the sermon? (for example, with a prayer)

- Where will you stand? Is there a pulpit? Are you expected to use it? Do you want to?

- Where can you put your notes, Bible, etc? Can you hold them, if you have to?

- How long is the sermon expected to last? (You should have checked this at an early stage in your planning)

You do not necessarily have to do what is normal in every instance, but it is better to know what is usual, and to only change it with good reason.

## How Do You Look?

Along with what we hear, we also take in a lot from what we see. When you preach, what your hearers can see should help, or at least not obstruct, what you have to say. Here are some points to bear in mind:

- **Dress:** Understand and respect your context. It does not help if what you wear distracts your hearers from what you are saying.

- **Posture:** If the way you sit or stand suggests that you are you are nervous or uncomfortable, that will communicate to your hearers.

- **Movement and gesture:** These can support and emphasize what you are saying. Individual styles will vary, but it probably best to avoid the extremes of being either a human statue or a human windmill! Also, bear in mind that when then is no good reason to move, it is usually best to be still, but to try and avoid putting your hands in your pockets.

- **Be yourself**—while also being aware of what is appropriate in your role and context.

## Making Yourself Heard

To state the obvious, the best prepared sermon in the world is of little use if it cannot be heard. Be sensitive to the size and type of building you are in, so that you are not too quiet, or too loud! Many churches now have sound systems, but they need to be used in the right way. If you are not sure how to use microphones well, then think about who you could ask.

We all have some relative weaknesses in the way we speak, so it is important to be aware of the faults you are most likely to slip into. We may avoid these faults when we are at our best, but they are likely to re-emerge when we are tired, distracted or ill at ease. Some of us may tend to speak too quickly, or too slowly, or not pronounce certain sounds very clearly. A dull, monotonous voice, or one with very exaggerated expression, can be hard to listen to. I have learnt that my own pitfall is to drop my voice at the end of a phrase or sentence. While we have to preach 'in role,' and will not speak in exactly the same way as we would in other more informal settings, it is important to speak with our own voice, and not in a forced or artificial way.

---

*To Think About*

What are your habitual pitfalls in the way that you speak? If you are not sure, how can you find out?

Can you think of any way that you can get some help or advice, if you need it?

---

# Mind Your Language

The briefer your notes are, the more important it is to be aware of the language you are using as you preach. Even if you preach from a full text, you will still produce some spontaneous words and phrases as you deliver your sermon. The language in preaching can be creative and lively, but also needs to be clear, understandable, and appropriate to the context. Sentences that are too long, and specialized or 'jargon' words, can make it harder for listeners to follow you. There are sometimes good reasons to introduce specialized or unusual words in a sermon, but, if it is too distracting to explain them, it may be better to find an alternative word that will be more easily understood.

In recent years, those who write or revise liturgical texts have become more sensitive to the need for 'inclusive language.'[8] This means trying to use terms that do not exclude or offend groups of people, for example, using words such as 'people' or 'humanity' rather than 'men' or 'mankind,' when we *mean* all people. The same concern applies to the words we use to describe older or younger people, racial or ethnic groups, people with disabilities, and so on. While there may be occasions when we inadvertently give offence, care in the language we use is part of our care for others, and I do not think it is possible to dismiss this concern as 'political correctness.' Any place where we can choose the words we use to refer to other people, as we do in preaching, is a position of power, and with that power comes the responsibility to use it with care, and not to place unnecessary obstacles in the way of others.

> ### To Think About
>
> Have you ever consciously changed the way you refer to any group of people? What was it that prompted that change?
>
> Are you aware of anything you should think about changing now?

## What Happens Next?

Preaching seeks a response from the hearers. In the next chapter we will look at personal comments and responses about the preacher, but here we will look at the question of responses to the content of a sermon, either within or immediately following the service.

The aim that you set out in your preparation will itself suggest a kind of response that you are hoping for, sometimes very clearly. A classic example is the evangelistic sermon, followed by an invitation to make or renew a commitment to Christ by standing up, or coming forward, or seeking prayer. There are many other possibilities,[9] of which these are a few examples:

- A sermon about stewardship, followed by an invitation to pledge a gift, or regular giving, to church, missions, charities, or other causes.

- A sermon about God's forgiveness, followed by a particular focus on confession and assurance of forgiveness, either as a congregation or for individuals.

- A sermon about healing, followed by the offer of individual prayer ministry.

- A sermon about justice in global trade, followed by a stall selling fair trade goods, and information about campaigns, petitions and so on.

- A sermon about spiritual gifts, followed by waiting on God in prayer, and ministry.

- A sermon about discipleship in daily life, followed by displays about organizations, and information about opportunities to volunteer.

Clearly, such ideas as these need planning in advance and co-ordination with others in leadership and ministry. Not every sermon will need such a clear and focussed response, but it would be a pity to miss such opportunities when they arise. There is an understandable concern to avoid 'emotionalism,' which has been defined as 'the deliberate and calculated manipulation of the emotions by the speaker,'[10] but that should not make us shy away from the proper place of emotion in preaching and worship. If we are to offer our whole selves in worship, that will include having an openness to God meeting us through our feelings and emotions.

I said earlier that all of our planning is provisional, because it is dependent on God's blessing, guidance and correction. That is certainly true as we think about responses to preaching, and to keep this in mind can help us to guard against any inappropriate forms of manipulation. Whatever you have planned or intended, a passing comment or minor point in your sermon may have spoken powerfully to somebody, and prompted a response you had not envisaged, so be prepared for the unexpected. As the preacher, it is not necessarily your task to deal in depth with all approaches, but be ready to give an initial response, and know who you can refer people to, whether that is the vicar, a prayer or counselling team, or other individuals within the church.

Having said all this, there will be times when we will see no obvious response to our preaching amongst our hearers, and we will have to trust that God has sown seeds that others may see the fruits of in the future.

# Reflecting and Learning 6

*The nature of Christian discipleship and ministry is to be always ready to learn, and our experiences can be a rich resource for learning.*

After you have preached you may well get some comments and responses from members of the congregation, and you can choose to invite and encourage them. Some comments will be no more than a brief thank-you, but others can be more significant. It is worth thinking a little about how to deal with different kinds of personal response to your preaching. If you are offered praise and compliments, will you hear them and accept them gratefully, or will you be embarrassed and deflect them with a joke? If someone is unnecessarily negative and rude, how will you deal with that, and how could you find support from others if you need it?

It can be helpful to have some structured opportunities for response. Some training courses ask for this to be done, but it can be useful for experienced preachers as well. On the next page we set out a possible framework for written evaluation of a sermon.[11] For convenience it is set out here on an A5 sheet, but an A4 version with more space for comments is available for download on the Grove web site. You may know of other feedback forms, or you could take and adapt this one to suit your situation. I believe it is better to keep such forms fairly brief, preferably on one side of a sheet of paper, but invite additional comments if people want to add them. They can be offered to a whole congregation, but not everybody has the gift of offering helpful and constructive criticism, and it can be difficult to deal with a very negative response, especially if you do not have any support or guidance in interpreting it. With modern technology it is also a realistic possibility to tape, and now to video, your preaching, for you to review afterwards.

It is also possible to invite particular people to give you feedback. John Leach has suggested an interesting system of 'feedback partners' in which a team of worship leaders each give feedback to one another.[12] This has the advantage that all those who give feedback are experienced in the same field, and over time will be receiving as well as giving it. The same pattern could be used amongst a team or group of preachers, so long as they are able to hear one another preach, which is not always easy when resources are stretched in situations such as a multi-parish rural benefice.

---

# Sermon Evaluation

Preacher:  Date and time:

Church:  Type of service:

Subject:


## Sermon Content

1 What do you think was the aim of the sermon?
2 Did you sense a structure or direction in the sermon?
3 How were the Bible readings used in the sermon?
4 Where was 'good news' to be found in the sermon?
5 How well was the sermon illustrated with examples and stories?
6 How well was the sermon related to everyday life and practical issues?
7 How far did the sermon challenge your mind, and stir your emotions?
8 How well did the sermon fit into the service as a whole?

## Sermon Delivery

1 Could you hear the preacher?
2 Were the opening and closing prayers, if any, suitable?
3 How well did the preacher gain your attention at the start?
4 Were the language and ideas appropriate to the congregation?
5 How well did the preacher end the sermon?
6 Did anything about the preacher's dress, manner, voice or gestures particularly help or distract you?

## And Finally

1 What one thing would you encourage the preacher to keep doing as they are?
2 And what one thing would you encourage the preacher to work at and improve?

---

## Always Learning

This is equally true, whether we are just beginning, or have many years of experience, and it is true in preaching as in any other aspect of life and faith. One of the most fruitful ways to learn is by reflecting on our experience in a critical way, that is, with an open and questioning attitude. A very helpful pattern for this is the learning cycle developed by David Kolb, which has been summarized like this in a book aimed at preachers:[13]

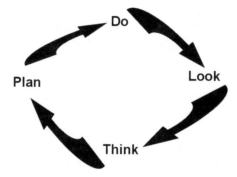

The great thing about this model is its flexibility. You can join the cycle at any stage, and it can be applied to any period of time, however long or short. It can also be pictured as a loop or spiral, for if you have done, looked (or remembered), thought, and then planned, your second action will be different from the first, giving the cycle a sense of movement and progression, rather than just repetition:

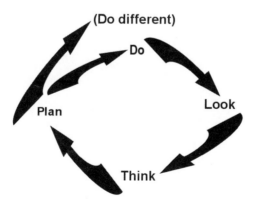

The terms in the cycle can also be made more specific to a particular activity, so a learning cycle for preachers might look like this:

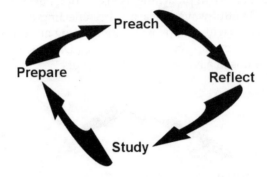

This can serve as a useful reminder to take some time to reflect on your previous preaching, and to use feedback and evaluation from others, as part of the process of continuing learning through experience. The four steps in the cycle will not always be very conscious, or take the same amount of time. There will be some studying in preparation for every sermon, at least in exploring the Bible readings, but there may also be other times of more intensive study, such as in reading a book about preaching, or going on a training or refresher course.

As with other tools for learning, this cycle is not to be used in a rigid or restrictive way, but it may be useful to help us understand what we have been doing, and to remind us of the importance of being open to new learning throughout a ministry in preaching.

# Further Reading and Resources 7

## Other 'How To...' Books in this Series

Anna de Lange and Liz Simpson, Grove Worship booklet W 169 *How to... Lead the Prayers: A Training Course*

Anna de Lange and Liz Simpson, Grove Worship booklet W 177 *How to...Read the Bible in Church: A Training Course*

## About Preaching

Charles Chadwick and Phillip Tovey, Grove Worship booklet W 164 *Developing Reflective Practice for Preachers*

D Coggan, *New Day for Preaching* (London: SPCK, 1987, 1996)

D Day, *A Preaching Workbook* (London: Lynx, 1998)

John Leach, Grove Worship booklet W 139 *Responding to Preaching*

E L Lowry, *The Homiletic Plot* (Atlanta: John Knox Press, 1980)

J R W Stott, *I Believe in Preaching* (London: Hodder and Stoughton, 1982)

Tim Stratford, Grove Worship booklet W 144 *Interactive Preaching: Opening the Word then Listening*

Phillip Tovey, Grove Worship booklet W 178 *Preaching a Sermon Series with Common Worship*

## About Preaching and Biblical Interpretation

Bob Fyall, Grove Biblical booklet B 4 *Preaching Old Testament Narrative*

John Proctor, Grove Biblical booklet B 9 *The Christmas Stories in Faith and Preaching*

Stephen Wright, Grove Biblical booklet B 20 *Preaching with the Grain of Scripture*

### Resources on the Internet

*Roots*, a series of bi-monthly magazine-style publications, offering lectionary-based resources for worship and preaching, available from Methodist Publishing House. Information and samples can be found at www.rootsontheweb.com

Back copies of Grove Books' quarterly *Biblical Studies Bulletin*, which includes regular surveys of commentaries on different books of the Bible, are now available through the web site at www.grovebooks.co.uk

# Notes

1   *Faith and Worship: Local Preachers Training Course 14, Preaching Good News* (Peterborough: Methodist Publishing House,1993), p 2 (referred to below as Preaching Good News).

2   Bernard L Manning, quoted in *Preaching Good News*, p 3.

3   *Preaching Good News*, p 3, attributes this to Colin Morris. A brief internet search suggests various possible sources, but it appears to have originally referred to the role of journalists.

4   *Preaching Good News*, p 4.

5   My thinking was stimulated by a simpler chart in *Preaching Good News*, p 4, and this chart was developed from that.

6   *Preaching Good News*, p 17.

7   *Common Worship* main book, pp 21, 27.

8   See, for example, M Earey and G Myers (ed), *Common Worship Today* (London: Harper Collins, 2001), p 83, 107.

9   See John Leach, Grove Worship booklet W 139 *Responding to Preaching*.

10   Preaching Good News, p 32.

11   Adapted from P Ballard and J Pritchard, *Practical Theology in Action* (London: SPCK, 1996), p 175–6.

12   J Leach, *Leading Worship That Connects: A training course* (London: Lynx, 1999), p 62–3.

13   Charles Chadwick and Phillip Tovey, Grove Worship booklet W 164 *Developing Reflective Practice for Preachers*.